"Poems that Win"

TAMARA LOFTON

Copyright © 2023 Tamara Lofton.

All rights reserved. No part of this book may be reproduced, stored, or transmitted by any means—whether auditory, graphic, mechanical, or electronic—without written permission of both publisher and author, except in the case of brief excerpts used in critical articles and reviews. Unauthorized reproduction of any part of this work is illegal and is punishable by law.

ISBN: 979-8-89031-764-3 (sc)
ISBN: 979-8-89031-765-0 (hc)
ISBN: 979-8-89031-766-7 (e)

Because of the dynamic nature of the Internet, any web addresses or links contained in this book may have changed since publication and may no longer be valid. The views expressed in this work are solely those of the author and do not necessarily reflect the views of the publisher, and the publisher hereby disclaims any responsibility for them.

One Galleria Blvd., Suite 1900, Metairie, LA 70001
(504) 702-6708

Dedication

It takes a village to raise a child.
It takes a village to shape by example.
It takes a village to promote good character.
It takes a village to stabilize integrity.
It takes a village to produce a leader.

The eagles in my life shaped me and taught me to soar.

Although bruised along the way,
they displayed their scars as trophies of honor.

Consistently engaging in the good fight of faith,
They realized that "winners never
quit and quitters never win!

They recognized His voice.
They responded to His call.

They responsibly completed each ordained assignment,
teaching me to do the same.

Love YA!

Contents

The Assignment 7

"My Attitude" 10

"Courage" 12

"Practice" 14

"A Cooperative Response" 15

"Temperature Control" 17

"Preparation" 19

"Responsibility" 20

"Progress" 21

"From Challenge To Victory" 22

"Listen To The Leading" 24

The Assignment

An assignment is an appointed task,
To fulfill the Great Commission.

With a pre-ordained charge,
He will lovingly ask,
then proceed to place you in position.

The purpose of the mission determines the placement,
in spite of your present condition.

After opposition, trials, adjustments, and tests,
the prep will upgrade your position.

The mission is sure,
The responsibility is great.

The potential for discomfort,
The burden carries an eternal weight.

The call to salvation,
His mission to all.

He gave his own life,
To prevent man's eternal fall.

And then at the end,
He will call you to rest.

Enter into His kingdom!
Sit at His feet and be blessed!

"My Attitude"

My attitude influences my mindset.

My mindset determines my approach.

My approach has the potential to settle a dispute,

or to completely dismantle a peaceful solution.

"Courage"

A courage to stand,

A courage to endure,

A courage that is reckless, empowering, and sure.

Tenacity, audacity, gallantry, and guts,

Be thou strong and very courageous.

Assume the posture,

No *if*, *ands*, or *buts*!

"Practice"

Practice makes improvement.

Improvement strengthens the ability.

Consistent maturity breeds excellence.

Completed excellence produces perfection.

"A Cooperative Response"

To live, to love, and then receive,
achieve success and grow.
Develop fully in His word, together we can flow.

Forgive, forget, release, let go, all stressful discontent.
And be assured amidst the trial,
to rest upon His strength.

Possess the fullness of His love and
cherish routes unknown.
For in the storm and through the
flood, you will not be alone.

To know, to stay, to fight, to prove,
to rest unchanged and calm.
Uncertain times and tests of will,
can't shake His peaceful balm.

"Temperature Control"

You are not a Thermometer;
an instrument that merely registers the temperature.

You are a Thermostat;
the device that automatically adjusts the temperature
to a desired level.

Living things grow!
Growing things change!

You have been called to set the tone,
formulate the atmosphere,
orchestrate the mood,
maintain the temperature!

You are the example.
You are the "Instrument of Change."

If it does not exist,
Then you must create it to be!

"Preparation"

Preparation is a safeguard, a precaution, and a plan,
that will train, alert, and mold you,
while pursuing His divine plan.

Construction, and formation, education, expectation,
reinforced determination,
as you build on a solid foundation.

"Responsibility"

Responsibility is more than an obligated sense of duty.
It is a trusted example of accountability,
that blooms into a beautiful bouquet
of seasoned maturity.

"Progress"

To progress forward,
one must have a sense of what has been.

To progress onward,
One must release what is restricting the progression.

To stay focused,
One must determine truth from error.

To advance,
One must stay on course.

"From Challenge To Victory"

Challenges, Trouble, Trials, and Tests,
Obstacles, Hindrances, Road Blocks,
What's Next?

Detours and Sidetracks assigned to your life,
Assigned to your route, course, and path,
Such a Fight!

Without a test, there would be no fight
Without a fight, there would be no battle.

With no official battle, there could be no victory.
To void the victory, would never yield a conquest.

Without a conquest, there could be no possession.
Fight, Possess, and Win!

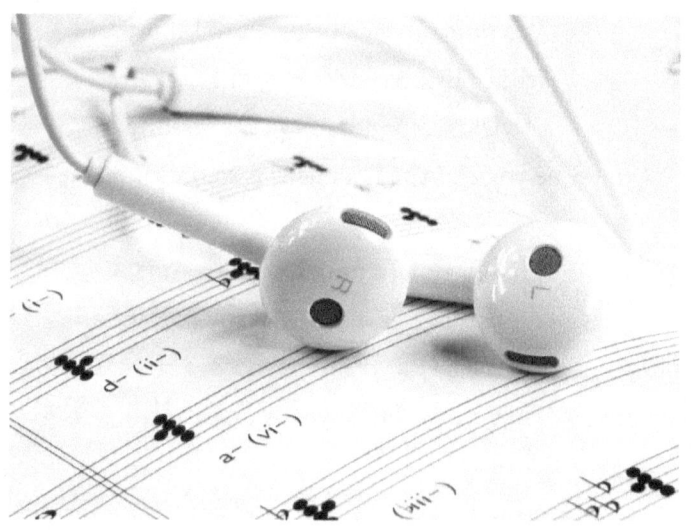

"Listen To The Leading"

We must allow our heart to know,
Within His presence, His will can flow.
To yield, respond, His grace abound,
The voice of the Shepherd is so profound.

His sheep will only follow the one,
God sent from heaven, Jesus Christ His Son.
They know His voice, they know His call,
They know His love for one and all.

For God is not the author of confusion.
To those who wander, this is an illusion.
Confusion, diversion, an adverse reaction,
The voice of a stranger is such a distraction.

Elijah, the witness to a phenomenal occurrence,
No answer in the wind, earthquake, or fire,
Such a terrible disturbance!

Choose to hear Him patiently,
In His still small voice applaud.
So quiet yourself, be still and know,
That He alone is God!

TAMARA LOFTON

Former Educator/Musician/Tutor/Life Long Learner

"Whatever she learns her
response is to teach"....

Tamenterprises
PO Box 239
Stone Mtn, GA 30186

tamrhythmic@yahoo.com

https://www.tamrhythmic.com/

www.ingramcontent.com/pod-product-compliance
Lightning Source LLC
LaVergne TN
LVHW092103060526
838201LV00047B/1543